Heroes All Around Us

3 4 5 6 7 8 9 10   050   13 12 11 10 09 08

SCHOOL PUBLISHERS

Visit *The Learning Site!* www.harcourtschool.com

Heroes Come from Many Places

READ TO FIND OUT **What kinds of people are heroes?**

A **hero** is a person who does something important. Heroes have strong beliefs. They make things happen. Heroes are brave. People look up to them.

Abigail Duniway was a hero to her family. In 1862, her husband was hurt in an accident. She worked to earn money while caring for her family. She also worked for women's rights.

Abigail Duniway ran a newspaper and wrote a book about women's rights.

People who play sports can be heroes, too. Sometimes, they play even when they are in pain. They do all they can to win.

Babe Didrikson Zaharias was known for playing sports. Then she became sick. She did not let this stop her. After Babe got better, she went back to playing.

READING CHECK ŏ **MAIN IDEA AND DETAILS** What kinds of people are heroes?

Babe Didrikson Zaharias was a hero.

American Heroes

READ TO FIND OUT How can people be heroes in times of war?

In 1814, the United States was at war. The enemy wanted to destroy the White House. There were many beautiful and important things inside. Dolley Madison, the President's wife, made sure that some of those things were saved. She left before the White House was set on fire.

Dolley Madison saved a painting of George Washington.

Dorie Miller learned how to fire the gun by watching others do it.

In 1941, the United States was in another war. United States navy ships were attacked. On one ship, a machine-gun operator was killed. Dorie Miller, who worked in the ship's kitchen, quickly took his place. He shot down four enemy planes.

Dorie Miller had never fired a machine gun until that day. The navy gave him a medal for bravery. He was a hero.

READING CHECK **GENERALIZATION** **How can people be heroes in times of war?**

Heroes from Around the World

READ TO FIND OUT How do heroes change things?

Anna Sewell was a writer from England. She wrote a book called *Black Beauty*. She was sick as she worked on it, but the book was important to her.

Anna Sewell loved horses. She wanted people to treat horses kindly. She wrote *Black Beauty* to change how people thought about horses. Her book did change people's minds.

Many people still read *Black Beauty*.

When Simón Bolívar was a young man, he decided to one day make South America free.

Simón Bolívar was a South American general. He wanted to drive the Spanish out of South America. Bolívar fought for freedom for his people. He led his army against the Spanish many times. Finally, in 1825, South America was free.

The country of Bolivia is named after Simón Bolívar. Bolívar became known as the George Washington of South America.

READING CHECK **GENERALIZE How do heroes change things?**

Dolores Huerta

READ TO FIND OUT **How did Huerta bring about change?**

In the past, farmworkers were not treated fairly. They were paid little. Their children were hungry. The workers wanted their lives to be better.

Dolores Huerta was a teacher. She taught the children of farmworkers. She wanted to help the farmworkers change the way they were treated.

Dolores Huerta worked with Cesar Chavez to help farmworkers.

Dolores Huerta believed in nonviolence and called for boycotts.

Huerta believed in nonviolent actions to get people's attention. **Nonviolence** is the practice of not using violence to meet a goal. Huerta led many marches to help the workers.

Huerta and the workers called for boycotts of certain products. A **boycott** is a time when people stop buying a good or service. Laws were made to help the farmworkers. They were treated better.

`READING CHECK` ŏ **MAIN IDEA AND DETAILS How did Huerta bring about change?**

Harriet Tubman

READ TO FIND OUT **How did Harriet Tubman show courage?**

Harriet Tubman was born in Maryland in about 1820. During this time, many people still had slaves. Harriet wanted to escape from slavery and be free.

Harriet Tubman got help from the Underground Railroad. The Underground Railroad was not a real railroad. People known as conductors helped her find safe places to stay. A **conductor** was a person who helped enslaved people escape.

After she escaped, Harriet Tubman helped others on the Underground Railroad.

This painting shows people on the Underground Railroad.

Harriet Tubman later became the most famous conductor on the Underground Railroad. She went back to Maryland 19 times to help others escape.

Some people let Harriet Tubman hide in their houses. Other people wanted to stop her. She was never caught. She led many people to freedom.

READING CHECK GENERALIZE **How did Harriet Tubman show courage?**

Sacagawea

READ TO FIND OUT How did Sacagawea help Lewis and Clark?

An **explorer** is someone who travels to a new place. Meriwether Lewis and William Clark were explorers. Their job was to find out about new lands.

Lewis and Clark needed an interpreter to help them talk to the American Indians. An **interpreter** is someone who speaks more than one language and talks for people.

Sacagawea is honored with a statue.

Sacagawea with Lewis and Clark

They found an interpreter to go west with them. Her name was Sacagawea.

Sacagawea helped the explorers on the long, hard trip. She helped them talk with American Indians. Sometimes she told them which was the best way to go. Lewis and Clark named many places along the way after Sacagawea.

READING CHECK ŏ **MAIN IDEA AND DETAILS** How did Sacagawea help Lewis and Clark?

Heroes from Stories

READ TO FIND OUT Why do people make up stories about heroes?

Some heroes live only in stories. Long ago, the Greek people told stories about Prometheus (pruh·MEE·thee·us). He stole fire from the gods to give it to the people.

The angry gods tied Prometheus to a rock. Only another hero could save him. His name was Hercules (HER·kyoo·leez). He was the strongest man on Earth.

Only Hercules was strong enough to save Prometheus.

The first comic book about Superman came out in 1938.

People today make up stories about heroes. Sometimes the stories appear in comic books. Superman was one of the first comic book heroes. People liked reading about how Superman won battles against bad people.

Heroes in stories show people how to be brave. They give real people hope.

READING CHECK **CAUSE AND EFFECT** **Why do people make up stories about heroes?**

Johnny Appleseed

READ TO FIND OUT How was John Chapman like Johnny Appleseed?

Johnny Appleseed was a hero who often appeared in stories. The stories said that Johnny gave people apple seeds. Pictures showed him carrying a bag of seeds and wearing no shoes.

Not all of this was true. Johnny Appleseed was a real man. His name was John Chapman.

Johnny Appleseed has been in many books.

This is how John Chapman might have looked.

John Chapman did love apple trees. In 1797, he went west. He took apple seeds with him. Along the way, he planted the seeds.

When other people came to live in the West, they found Johnny's trees. This is why he was called Johnny Appleseed. People made up stories about how he planted all the seeds.

READING CHECK **COMPARE AND CONTRAST** How was John Chapman like Johnny Appleseed?

The Legend of Tan-Gun

READ TO FIND OUT **What makes the story of Tan-gun a legend?**

A **legend** is a made-up story about a real person. Some parts may be true. Other parts are not. It is hard to tell which parts of a legend are real.

The story of Tan-gun is a legend. This is how it begins. "Long, long ago, a bear changed into a woman. The bear-woman had a son named Tan-gun, who founded the kingdom of Choson."

Tan-gun's birthday is a holiday for school children in Korea.

People honor Tan-gun by visiting the place he is believed to be buried.

Tan-gun's story tells how he became a great leader. He was both brave and wise. His kingdom became the country of Korea.

Today, many people in Korea think of themselves as the children of Tan-gun. To them, he is a hero. His story makes them feel proud of their country. They hope to be brave and wise like Tan-gun.

READING CHECK **GENERALIZE** **What makes the story of Tan-gun a legend?**

Activity 1

Write a word from the list to complete each sentence.

hero	explorer	nonviolence
interpreter	boycott	legend
conductor		

1. Many people stopped buying grapes because of a _____ by farmworkers.

2. If you cannot understand another language, an _____ can help you.

3. My grandfather told me the _____ of Tan-gun.

4. Many people called the brave firefighter a _____.

5. The _____ went into a cave to find out what was there.

6. A peaceful person believes in _____.

7. Harriet Tubman was a _____ on the Underground Railroad.

Activity 2

Look at the list of terms. Categorize the terms in a chart like the one below. Then use a dictionary to learn the definitions of the terms you do not know.

hero	explorer	nonviolence
interpreter	boycott	legend
ancient	civil rights	explorer
fictional	folktale	freedom
holiday	independence	natural resource
pioneers	region	settlement
tall tale	conductor	

		I Know	Sounds Familiar	Don't Know
○	legend			✓
	nonviolence		✓	
	explorer	✓		

Activity 3

Match each term to its meaning.

hero   legend   explorer

interpreter   boycott   nonviolence

conductor

1. peaceful ways to change things that are not fair

2. a made-up story about a real person

3. a person who goes to find out about a place

4. a decision to stop buying or using certain things

5. a brave person who does something important

6. a person who helped others escape slavery

7. a person who knows more than one language and helps other people talk

Activity 4

Write the definition for each word. Then use each word in a sentence.

1. hero

2. nonviolence

3. boycott

4. interpreter

5. explorer

6. legend

7. conductor

Review

 Main Idea and Details What kinds of people are heroes?

Vocabulary

1. What is a **legend**?

Recall

2. How did Dolores Huerta help farmworkers?

3. What did John Chapman do?

4. Who was a famous conductor on the Underground Railroad?

Critical Thinking

5. How can stories about heroes help people?

Activity

Write a Paragraph Think about a person you feel is a hero. Write a paragraph about him or her. Explain what makes the person a hero. Share your paragraph with the class.

Photo Credits Front cover: © Bill Stormont/Corbis; 2, CORBIS; 3, Bettmann/CORBIS; 4, Collection of the New York Historical Society; 5, Courtesy of the US National Archives, Washington, DC, USA; 6(bl), Mary Evans Picture Library/Alamy; 6(br), Mary Evans Picture Library/Alamy; 7, Atwater Kent Museum of Philadelphia; 8, David Young-Wolff; 9, Bob Fitch/TakeStock; 10, Library of Congress; 12, John Elk; 13, "Lewis and Clark at Three Forks" by E.S. Paxson, Oil on Canvas 1912, Courtesy of the Montana Historical Society, Don Beatty photographer; 14, The Art Archive/Museo Nazionale Palazzo Altemps Rome/Dagli Orti; 15, SuperStock, Inc./SuperStock; 18, The Bridgeman Art Library; 19, Walter L. Keats